QUOTES FOR COACHES

A WEEKLY JOURNAL OF QUOTES TO INSPIRE LEADERSHIP, BUILD CHAMPIONS AND DRIVE PERFORMANCE

THE QUOTIVATION SERIES

DR. JO LUKINS

ISBN: 978-1-7635127-6-4 (Paperback)

Elite Edge Publishing

www.drjolukins.com

Quotes for Coaches invites you to explore wisdom from those who have achieved in sports, business, politics, the military, and as thought leaders; thoughtfully selected to support your journey. Set aside time each week to reflect on the quote and consider what it means for you. A diary entry or reminder can help you stay committed.

This journal offers space for your weekly reflections. As you consider each quote, notice which ones resonate and which ones you might question. Both reactions help you better understand your values and approach to performance.

The second part of the book provides further reflection questions. These are designed to give you space for your own thoughts before considering additional prompts.

Looking for some extra accountability to keep you inspired throughout the year?

You can choose to receive a weekly email with each quote and the journal prompts to help you stay motivated and on track. If you'd like to receive a weekly reminder, simply scan the QR code below and you'll start getting an email with the latest quote to help you move closer to your goals.

The quotes are organised into five key areas of successful coaching. If you have a particular area you'd like to focus on, use the guide below to find relevant quotes.

TEAMWORK, CULTURE AND TRUST

Quotes: 3, 5, 7, 9, 15, 22, 23, 26, 28, 29, 35, 39, 43, 45

STANDARDS, DETAIL AND PREPARATION

Quotes: 4, 6, 8, 19, 21, 25, 27, 30, 37, 38, 42, 50, 51, 52

LEADERSHIP, MOTIVATION AND TEACHING

Quotes: 1, 18, 33, 34, 44, 46, 48, 49

RESILIENCE, MINDSET AND MENTAL TOUGHNESS

Quotes: 10, 11, 14, 20, 31, 32, 40, 41

GROWTH, SELF-IMPROVEMENT AND GOALS

Quotes: 2, 12, 13, 16, 17, 24, 36, 47

Reflect and Perform

Each page offers a quote to spark reflection about your coaching mindset, routines, and team dynamics. Take your time, revisit the quote over a week, and observe how your views might change with ongoing experience.

Some quotes may be familiar, but their true value comes from thoughtful reflection. Consider how you might apply their message to make a lasting difference in your journey.

Performance-Driven Prompts

- After reflecting, what actions or habits could you apply this week in your business?
- If a quote feels at odds with your experience, notice what you believe instead, and make notes of your wisdom.

In the final section, you'll find space to add quotes you discover throughout the year, allowing your motivation to grow with you.

I look forward to sharing this journey. Reach out to let me know which quotes inspire you, and the impact they have on your performance and mindset. Shine bright, Dr. Jo (excel@drjolukins.com)

CUSTOM COPIES FOR YOUR TEAM OR SPORTING ORGANISATION. IF YOU'D LIKE YOUR OWN SET OF THE QUOTIVATION SERIES, PLEASE CONTACT US ABOUT CREATING A CUSTOM EDITION.

ONE

COACHING IS TAKING A PLAYER WHERE THEY CAN'T TAKE THEMSELVES.

JOSE MOURINHO

PORTUGUESE FOOTBALL MANAGER KNOWN FOR
LEADING ELITE EUROPEAN CLUBS TO MAJOR TITLES.

TWO

> ## IF YOU'RE NOT MAKING MISTAKES, THEN YOU'RE NOT DOING ANYTHING. I'M POSITIVE THAT A DOER MAKES MISTAKES.

JOHN WOODEN

AMERICAN BASKETBALL COACH WHO LED UCLA TO A RECORD RUN OF NCAA CHAMPIONSHIPS AND CREATED THE PYRAMID OF SUCCESS.

THREE

WINNING AND CHAMPIONSHIPS ARE MEMORABLE BUT THEY COME FROM THE STRENGTH OF THE RELATIONSHIPS.

JIM CALHOUN

COLLEGE BASKETBALL COACH WHO GUIDED THE UNIVERSITY OF CONNECTICUT MEN'S TEAM TO MULTIPLE NATIONAL TITLES.

FOUR

> ## IN PRACTICE, IF YOU DON'T LIKE TO DO IT, IT IS PROBABLY GOOD FOR YOU.

D. COTRELL

COACH AND AUTHOR KNOWN FOR PRACTICAL INSIGHTS ON TRAINING AND PLAYER DEVELOPMENT.

WHEN YOU UNDERSTAND WHAT MOTIVATES EACH PLAYER AND CONNECT THEM TO EACH OTHER, THAT'S WHEN A TEAM BECOMES SPECIAL.

JILL ELLIS

COACH WHO LED THE UNITED STATES WOMEN'S NATIONAL SOCCER TEAM TO CONSECUTIVE FIFA WOMEN'S WORLD CUP VICTORIES.

> # IF YOU THINK SMALL THINGS DON'T MATTER, THINK OF THE LAST GAME YOU LOST BY ONE POINT.
>
> ## UNKNOWN
>
> POPULAR ANONYMOUS COACHING QUOTE HIGHLIGHTING HOW SMALL DETAILS DECIDE CLOSE CONTESTS.

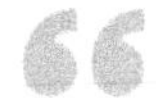

SEVEN

MY RESPONSIBILITY IS GETTING ALL MY PLAYERS PLAYING FOR THE NAME ON THE FRONT OF THE JERSEY, NOT THE ONE ON THE BACK.

UNKNOWN

ANONYMOUS QUOTE OFTEN USED TO EMPHASISE TEAM IDENTITY OVER INDIVIDUAL RECOGNITION.

THE DIFFERENCE BETWEEN AN EXTRAORDINARY PLAYER AND AN ORDINARY PLAYER IS THAT LITTLE EXTRA.

MICHAEL BURKS

COACH AND COMMENTATOR ASSOCIATED WITH
MESSAGES ABOUT EFFORT AND EXCELLENCE.

GREAT TEAMS ARE BUILT ON RELATIONSHIPS. YOU WIN BECAUSE YOU CARE ABOUT ONE ANOTHER ENOUGH TO HOLD EACH OTHER ACCOUNTABLE.

PAT SUMMITT

UNIVERSITY OF TENNESSEE WOMEN'S BASKETBALL COACH AND ONE OF THE MOST SUCCESSFUL COACHES IN COLLEGE HISTORY.

NEITHER CRITICISM NOR PRAISE SHOULD BE HIGHLY REGARDED.

TEX WINTER

BASKETBALL COACH WHO DEVELOPED THE TRIANGLE OFFENSE AND ASSISTED ON MULTIPLE NBA CHAMPIONSHIP TEAMS.

WE MAY ENCOUNTER MANY DEFEATS, BUT WE MUST NOT BE DEFEATED.

MAYA ANGELOU

AMERICAN POET, MEMOIRIST AND CIVIL RIGHTS
ACTIVIST KNOWN FOR HER WRITING ON RESILIENCE
AND IDENTITY.

PERSISTENCE CAN CHANGE FAILURE INTO EXTRAORDINARY ACHIEVEMENT.

MATT BIONDI

AMERICAN SWIMMER AND MULTIPLE OLYMPIC GOLD MEDALLIST.

> # THE PRINCIPLE IS COMPETING AGAINST YOURSELF. IT'S ABOUT SELF-IMPROVEMENT, ABOUT BEING BETTER THAN YOU WERE THE DAY BEFORE.
>
> **STEVE YOUNG**
> HALL OF FAME QUARTERBACK WHO LED THE SAN FRANCISCO 49ERS TO A SUPER BOWL TITLE.

THE IDEA IS NOT TO BLOCK EVERY SHOT. THE IDEA IS TO MAKE YOUR OPPONENT BELIEVE THAT YOU MIGHT BLOCK EVERY SHOT.

BILL RUSSELL

BOSTON CELTICS GREAT WHO WON 11 NBA CHAMPIONSHIPS AND LATER COACHED AT THE PROFESSIONAL LEVEL.

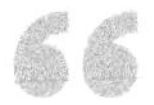

FIFTEEN

THE CHEMISTRY HAS TO START WITH TRUST. IF THEY DON'T TRUST YOU AND THEY DON'T TRUST EACH OTHER, YOU DON'T HAVE A TEAM, YOU JUST HAVE A GROUP.

DAWN STALEY

OLYMPIC GOLD MEDALLIST AND HEAD COACH OF THE UNIVERSITY OF SOUTH CAROLINA WOMEN'S BASKETBALL PROGRAM.

SETTING A GOAL IS NOT THE MAIN THING. IT IS DECIDING HOW YOU WILL GO ABOUT ACHIEVING IT AND STAYING WITH THAT PLAN.

TOM LANDRY

LONG-TIME DALLAS COWBOYS HEAD COACH KNOWN FOR INNOVATION AND TWO SUPER BOWL WINS.

WHAT TO DO WITH A MISTAKE, RECOGNIZE IT, ADMIT IT, LEARN FROM IT, FORGET IT.

DEAN SMITH

UNIVERSITY OF NORTH CAROLINA MEN'S BASKETBALL COACH AND MENTOR TO MANY FUTURE NBA PLAYERS.

TO TEACH IS TO LEARN TWICE.

JOSEPH JOUBERT

FRENCH WRITER REMEMBERED FOR HIS CONCISE, REFLECTIVE MAXIMS.

> # WE ARE WHAT WE REPEATEDLY DO. EXCELLENCE, THEREFORE, IS NOT AN ACT BUT A HABIT.

ARISTOTLE

ANCIENT GREEK PHILOSOPHER WHOSE WORK SHAPED WESTERN IDEAS ABOUT ETHICS, LOGIC AND SCIENCE.

IF YOU'RE AFRAID TO FAIL, YOU'LL NEVER DO THE THINGS YOU'RE CAPABLE OF DOING.

JEN WELTER

AMERICAN FOOTBALL COACH WHO BECAME THE FIRST
WOMAN TO COACH IN THE NFL.

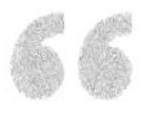

TWENTY-ONE

THE SMALLER THE DETAIL, THE GREATER THE VALUE.

DOUG JOHNSON

COACH AND PERFORMANCE COMMENTATOR WHO
STRESSES PRECISION AND ATTENTION TO DETAIL.

TWENTY-TWO

> YOU CAN HAVE ALL THE TALENT IN THE WORLD, BUT IF YOU DON'T HAVE A GROUP THAT'S WILLING TO WORK FOR EACH OTHER, YOU WON'T WIN MUCH.

SARINA WIEGMAN

FOOTBALL MANAGER WHO HAS WON MAJOR INTERNATIONAL TITLES WITH THE NETHERLANDS AND ENGLAND WOMEN'S NATIONAL TEAMS.

TWENTY-THREE

WINNING IS ABOUT HAVING THE WHOLE TEAM ON THE SAME PAGE.

BILL WALTON

HALL OF FAME BASKETBALL CENTRE AND
COMMENTATOR KNOWN FOR HIS VIEWS ON TEAMWORK.

TWENTY-FOUR

EACH SETBACK IS A LESSON. THE ONLY REAL FAILURE IS NOT LEARNING FROM IT.

CATHY FREEMAN

AUSTRALIAN 400-METRE CHAMPION AND OLYMPIC
GOLD MEDALLIST.

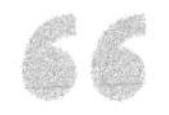

CHAMPIONS ARE BUILT IN PRACTICE. GAMES JUST REVEAL WHAT YOU'VE BEEN PRACTICING.

MUFFET MCGRAW

NOTRE DAME WOMEN'S BASKETBALL COACH WHO LED HER TEAMS TO MULTIPLE NCAA TITLES.

> ROWING IS THE ULTIMATE TEAM SPORT. IF ONE PERSON IS OUT OF SYNC, THE BOAT GOES NOWHERE. LIFE AND LEADERSHIP ARE THE SAME.

KATHERINE GRAINGER

BRITISH ROWER AND MULTIPLE OLYMPIC MEDALLIST.

TWENTY-SEVEN

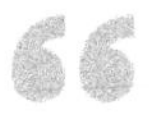

> DETAILS MATTER. IF WE'RE CASUAL IN THE SMALL THINGS, WE'LL BE CASUAL WHEN IT COUNTS.

SARAH ULMER

NEW ZEALAND CYCLIST AND OLYMPIC GOLD MEDALLIST.

YOU CAN ACCOMPLISH ANYTHING YOU WANT AS LONG AS YOU DON'T CARE WHO GETS THE CREDIT FOR IT.

BLANTON COLLIER

AMERICAN FOOTBALL COACH WHO LED THE CLEVELAND BROWNS TO AN NFL CHAMPIONSHIP.

WHEN THE LOCKER ROOM IS STRONG, THE SCOREBOARD USUALLY FOLLOWS.

BECKY HAMMON

FORMER WNBA PLAYER AND TRAILBLAZING COACH IN BOTH THE NBA AND WNBA.

IN GYMNASTICS, EVERY FINGER, EVERY TOE IS PART OF THE PERFORMANCE. THAT'S HOW I WANT MY TEAM TO THINK ABOUT THEIR HABITS.

SHANNON MILLER

ONE OF THE MOST DECORATED AMERICAN GYMNASTS
AND A MULTIPLE OLYMPIC MEDALLIST.

YOU DON'T ALWAYS CONTROL THE OUTCOME, BUT YOU ALWAYS CONTROL YOUR RESPONSE.

NICOLA ADAMS

BRITISH BOXER AND THE FIRST WOMAN TO WIN
OLYMPIC BOXING GOLD.

> # WE TOLD OUR RUNNERS TO HOLD ON FOR 30 MINUTES OF AGONY FOR 12 MONTHS OF GLORY.

JOHN MCDONNELL

UNIVERSITY OF ARKANSAS TRACK AND FIELD COACH WITH A RECORD HAUL OF NCAA CHAMPIONSHIPS.

FOR ME, COACHING IS ABOUT HELPING PEOPLE BELIEVE IN POSSIBILITIES THEY CAN'T YET SEE.

STACEY MARINKOVICH

AUSTRALIAN NETBALL COACH AND HEAD COACH OF THE NATIONAL DIAMONDS TEAM.

I TELL THE PLAYERS: YOUR LEGACY IS HOW YOU MAKE YOUR TEAMMATES BETTER.

TARA VANDERVEER

STANFORD UNIVERSITY WOMEN'S BASKETBALL COACH AND ONE OF THE WINNINGEST COACHES IN COLLEGE BASKETBALL.

YOU DON'T HAVE TO BE BEST FRIENDS, BUT YOU DO HAVE TO RESPECT EACH OTHER AND PLAY FOR EACH OTHER.

STACEY MARINKOVICH

NETBALL COACH KNOWN FOR BUILDING STRONG,
TEAM-FIRST ENVIRONMENTS WITH THE DIAMONDS AND
WEST COAST FEVER.

THINGS ARE NOT GOING TO GET EASIER. YOU ARE GOING TO HANDLE HARD BETTER.

KARA LAWSON

FORMER WNBA PLAYER AND CURRENT HEAD COACH OF DUKE UNIVERSITY WOMEN'S BASKETBALL.

FOCUS ON DOING THE NEXT THING RIGHT; THE SCORE TAKES CARE OF ITSELF.

LISA ALEXANDER

FORMER HEAD COACH OF THE AUSTRALIAN DIAMONDS NETBALL TEAM, WINNING MULTIPLE WORLD AND COMMONWEALTH TITLES.

THE ABSOLUTE BOTTOM LINE IN COACHING IS ORGANIZATION AND PREPARING FOR PRACTICE.

BILL WALSH

NFL COACH WHO BUILT THE SAN FRANCISCO 49ERS DYNASTY AND POPULARISED THE WEST COAST OFFENSE.

WE WIN WHEN 'I' BECOMES 'WE' IN EVERY CONVERSATION, EVERY HUDDLE, EVERY TRAINING SESSION.

CARLA OVERBECK

FORMER CAPTAIN OF THE U.S. WOMEN'S NATIONAL SOCCER TEAM AND LATER A COACH.

PRESSURE IS A PRIVILEGE. IT ONLY COMES TO THOSE WHO EARN IT.

MIKE KRZYZEWSKI

DUKE UNIVERSITY MEN'S BASKETBALL COACH WHO ALSO LED USA BASKETBALL TO MULTIPLE OLYMPIC GOLD MEDALS.

> # NEGATIVITY CAN SLIP INTO YOUR DAILY ACTIVITIES, BUT A POSITIVE ATTITUDE WILL WIN YOUR BATTLES.

NICK BOLLETTIERI

TENNIS COACH WHO FOUNDED A FAMOUS ACADEMY AND WORKED WITH NUMEROUS WORLD-NUMBER-ONE PLAYERS.

THE LITTLE THINGS MAKE THE BIG THINGS HAPPEN.

HERB BROOKS

ICE HOCKEY COACH BEST KNOWN FOR LEADING THE
1980 U.S. OLYMPIC "MIRACLE ON ICE" TEAM.

A SUCCESSFUL TEAM BEATS WITH ONE HEART.

ALEX FERGUSON

SCOTTISH FOOTBALL MANAGER WHO TURNED
MANCHESTER UNITED INTO A DOMINANT,
TITLE-WINNING CLUB.

THE SECRET TO COACHING IS NOT WHAT YOU KNOW, BUT WHAT YOUR PLAYERS HAVE LEARNED.

RED AUERBACH

BOSTON CELTICS COACH AND EXECUTIVE WHO BUILT
ONE OF THE NBA'S GREAT DYNASTIES.

GOOD TEAMS BECOME GREAT ONES WHEN THE MEMBERS TRUST EACH OTHER ENOUGH TO SURRENDER THE 'ME' FOR THE 'WE'.

PHIL JACKSON

NBA COACH WHO WON CHAMPIONSHIPS WITH THE CHICAGO BULLS AND LOS ANGELES LAKERS USING A TEAM-CENTRED APPROACH.

COACHES WHO CAN OUTLINE PLAYS ON A BLACKBOARD ARE A DIME A DOZEN. THE ONES WHO WIN GET INSIDE THEIR PLAYERS AND MOTIVATE.

VINCE LOMBARDI

GREEN BAY PACKERS COACH WHOSE NAME IS ON THE SUPER BOWL TROPHY AND WHO SYMBOLISES DISCIPLINED EXCELLENCE.

EVERYBODY MAKES MISTAKES, THAT'S WHY THEY PUT ERASERS ON PENCILS.

TOMMY LASORDA

LONG-TIME LOS ANGELES DODGERS MANAGER AND
COLOURFUL AMBASSADOR FOR BASEBALL.

IF YOU COMMAND WISELY, YOU'LL BE OBEYED CHEERFULLY.

THOMAS FULLER

ENGLISH CLERGYMAN AND WRITER KNOWN FOR HIS COLLECTIONS OF PROVERBS.

THE MOST VALUABLE PLAYER IS THE ONE THAT MAKES THE MOST PLAYERS VALUABLE.

PEYTON MANNING

HALL OF FAME NFL QUARTERBACK AND SUPER BOWL WINNER WITH THE COLTS AND BRONCOS.

EVERYONE WANTS TO WIN, BUT NOT EVERYONE IS WILLING TO PREPARE TO WIN.

BOBBY KNIGHT

INDIANA UNIVERSITY BASKETBALL COACH KNOWN FOR
HIS DEMANDING STYLE AND THREE NCAA TITLES.

IF YOU DON'T HAVE TIME TO DO IT RIGHT, WHEN WILL YOU HAVE TIME TO DO IT OVER?

JOHN WOODEN

UCLA BASKETBALL COACH WHOSE TEACHINGS ON CHARACTER AND PREPARATION INFLUENCED GENERATIONS OF COACHES.

HARD WORK BEATS TALENT WHEN TALENT DOESN'T WORK HARD.

TIM NOTKE

HIGH SCHOOL BASKETBALL COACH OFTEN CREDITED WITH THIS WELL-KNOWN MAXIM ON EFFORT AND TALENT.

You'll find my reflection questions in the following section. They've been included separately so you can first explore your own ideas and see what stands out to you.

This is your opportunity to stretch your thinking, challenge your habits, and connect each concept to your training and performance in a real and personal way.

Once you've completed your initial reflections, take a moment to read through the additional questions. See what sparks your curiosity or pushes you to think differently. Go back to your earlier notes and build on them; this is where real growth happens.

This process is designed to help you get the most from your reflections and keep your focus on progress, not perfection. Your effort in this space will be reflected in how you show up in your leadership and your life.

DR. JO

ONE

> Coaching is taking a player where they can't take themselves.

JOSE MOURINHO

Highlights the coach's role in stretching athletes beyond what they can reach alone, and seeing potential they can't yet.

- Where are you currently asking an athlete or group to go that they would not choose on their own?
- How do you challenge attainable improvement?
- What is one way you could better communicate the future you see for an athlete or team?

TWO

> If you're not making mistakes, then you're not doing anything. I'm positive that a doer makes mistakes.

JOHN WOODEN

Reminds us that mistakes are evidence of effort, not signals to stop, and that learning-focused environments help taking risks and growth.

- How do your athletes know it is safe to make mistakes?
- When did you last model owning and learning from one of your own errors?
- What could you change in training design to reward smart risk-taking, not just outcomes?

THREE

> Winning and championships are memorable but they come from the strength of the relationships.

JIM CALHOUN

Underlines that success is built on connection, trust and care. Strong relationships support honest feedback, accountability and resilience.

- How intentional are you about building relationships?
- Where in your squad or group are relationship stresses?
- What small relational habit could you build into each week to strengthen trust?

FOUR

> In practice, if you don't like to do it, it is probably good for you.

D. COTRELL

Emphasises leaning into uncomfortable work as that is where growth lives. Resisted drills and habits often separate average from excellent.

- Which drills or habits do your athletes resist that you know are good for them?
- How can you explain the *why* behind those hard elements more clearly?
- What is one area where you also avoid the hard work you know you should do as a coach?

FIVE

> When you understand what motivates each player and connect them to each other, that's when a team becomes special.

JILL ELLIS

Points to the power of understanding individual drivers and weaving them into a shared purpose, thus creating a genuine team.

- How well do you understand your players motivators?
- How do you link individual goals with the team's goals?
- Where could you create more peer-to-peer connection for your players?

SIX

> If you think small things don't matter, think of the last game you lost by one point.

UNKNOWN

Margins are often tiny. The standards around *small* skills, habits and details frequently decide close contests.

- What small detail needs more priority?
- How do you review tight games with your athletes without blaming, yet still highlighting detail?
- What is one micro-habit you could install that might shift a small margin result?

SEVEN

> My responsibility is getting all my players playing for the name on the front of the jersey, not the one on the back.

UNKNOWN

Through identity and purpose, athletes can be anchored to something bigger than themselves and more willing to sacrifice.

- How clearly have you defined what the name on the front of the jersey stands for?
- Where does ego get in the way of team identity?
- What ritual or practice could reinforce *we* over *me*?

EIGHT

> The difference between an extraordinary player and an ordinary player is that little extra.

MICHAEL BURKS

The gap between talent and commitment, where the little extra often appears as unseen effort, added repetitions and quiet discipline.

- What does *little extra* look like in your sport?
- How do you notice and celebrate athletes who quietly go beyond what is required?
- Where could you model your own *little extra* in preparation or reflection?

NINE

> Great teams are built on relationships. You win because you care about one another enough to hold each other accountable.

Real care includes courageous conversations and shared responsibility for performance.

- How comfortable are you having performance conversations with athletes?
- How do you encourage athletes to hold each other to account?
- Where does *being nice* be getting in the way of feedback?

TEN

> Neither criticism nor praise should be highly regarded.

Aim to stay grounded regardless of outside opinion. Over-attachment to either criticism or praise can distract from the work required.

- How do you respond to the external swings of opinion?
- What messages do you send your athletes about handling praise after a win?
- What routines help you and your group refocus on process after both success and setbacks?

ELEVEN

> We may encounter many defeats, but we must not be defeated.

MAYA ANGELOU

Reminds us that setbacks are inevitable in sport, but giving up is optional. The interpretation of losses shapes what happens next.

- How do you currently frame losses and disappointments with your team?
- What actions have helped your team bounce back?
- What language could you use after a defeat that keeps standards high and spirits intact?

TWELVE

> Persistence can change failure into extraordinary achievement.

MATT BIONDI

Reinforces that persistence can transform early failures into later success, especially across long seasons and long careers.

- Where in your program is persistence being tested?
- How do you help athletes stay engaged when progress feels slow?
- What long-term story or vision could you share to remind them why persistence matters?

THIRTEEN

> The principle is competing against yourself. It's about self-improvement, about being better than you were the day before.

STEVE YOUNG

Shifts focus from opponents to self-improvement, anchoring performance to personal standards and intrinsic motivation.

- How do you measure growth other than the scoreboard?
- What personal performance metrics could you use with athletes to track better than yesterday?
- Where might you be fuelling comparison rather than self-competition?

FOURTEEN

> The idea is not to block every shot. The idea is to make your opponent believe that you might block every shot.

BILL RUSSELL

Draws attention to psychological impact, where opponents respond not only to actions but to what they believe you might do.

- How do your training standards build culture?
- How does your team project confidence without arrogance?
- What habits increase your athletes' belief in themselves?

FIFTEEN

> The chemistry has to start with trust. If they don't trust you and they don't trust each other, you don't have a team, you just have a group.

DAWN STALEY

Stresses that trust is the foundation of any functioning group and that even talented squads remain individuals in uniform without it.

- Where is trust in you, between athletes, or with staff?
- What actions most quickly build or rebuild trust?
- How might you create space for more open sharing?

SIXTEEN

> Setting a goal is not the main thing. It is deciding how you will go about achieving it and staying with that plan.

TOM LANDRY

Insists that goals without a clear method are wishes, and that daily habits and structures turn intentions into progress.

- What are the plans to support your goals?
- How do your weekly sessions reflect the desired outcomes?
- What is one adjustment you could make to bring planning and execution into closer alignment?

SEVENTEEN

 What to do with a mistake, recognize it, admit it, learn from it, forget it.

DEAN SMITH

Offers a simple process for dealing with errors, helping athletes move from recognition to learning and then letting go.

- Denial, shame or moving on too quickly - what are the main risks for your athletes?
- What review process turns errors into learning?
- How might this four-step response be used in coaching?

EIGHTEEN

 To teach is to learn twice.

JOSEPH JOUBERT

Suggests that teaching deepens understanding, and that involving athletes in explaining or demonstrating skills strengthens both knowledge and leadership.

- How often do athletes in your environment teach or lead elements of training?
- Which concepts would become clearer if players had to explain them to teammates?
- What is one way you could share more teaching responsibility with your leaders?

NINETEEN

 We are what we repeatedly do. Excellence, therefore,
is not an act but a habit.

ARISTOTLE

Excellence is formed through repeated behaviors, and consistent standards in ordinary moments become identity on game day.

- What everyday habits in your program reflect excellence?
- What exceptions that quietly lower the bar?
- What one habit, if consistently upheld, would most improve your team's identity?

TWENTY

 If you're afraid to fail, you'll never do the things you're
capable of doing.

JEN WELTER

Challenges the fear that stops athletes discovering their full capacity and calls on coaches to normalise failure as part of progress.

- What messages do you give about failure in your environment, both spoken and unspoken?
- Which athlete currently needs more permission to be bold and make mistakes?
- How could your session design encourage experimentation instead of only safe choices?

TWENTY-ONE

 The smaller the detail, the greater the value.

DOUG JOHNSON

Tiny behaviors carry significant impact on performance and culture. Attending to details signal standards, care and professionalism.

- Which recurring detail in your program most clearly reflects your standards?
- Where have small things slid that now need attention?
- What is the next detail you will raise the standard on?

TWENTY-TWO

 You can have all the talent in the world, but if you don't have a group that's willing to work for each other, you won't win much.

SARINA WIEGMAN

Talent without connection rarely delivers when it matters. Success depends on players prioritising each other, before themselves.

- Where do you currently see talent that is not fully invested in the group?
- How do you reward behaviors that show athletes putting the team first?
- What conversations are needed to align talented individuals with the collective?

TWENTY-THREE

 Winning is about having the whole team on the same page.

BILL WALTON

How intentionally do I build shared understanding ensuring every team member knows the plan, their role, and the purpose driving it?

- How clearly do you communicate roles and expectations?
- Where do you notice confusion or mixed messages?
- What could you do in your next meeting or session to get everyone on the same page?

TWENTY-FOUR

 Each setback is a lesson. The only real failure is not learning from it.

CATHY FREEMAN

Invites a mindset that sees disappointment as data rather than failure. Growth requires extracting lessons rather than replaying mistakes.

- How do you currently review setbacks with your athletes: critically, constructively or not at all?
- What recent result still needs to be properly debriefed for learning?
- How might you build a consistent what did we learn? routine after tough moments?

TWENTY-FIVE

 Champions are built in practice. Games just reveal what you've been practicing.

MUFFET MCGRAW

Links outcomes directly to training habits, using competition as a mirror. Standards accepted in practice are the standards in pressure.

- Where is the gap between practice and game intensity?
- What training behaviors wouldn't you tolerate in games?
- How could you redesign sessions so they more honestly reflect game realities?

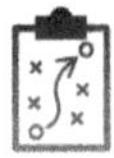

TWENTY-SIX

 Rowing is the ultimate team sport. If one person is out of sync, the boat goes nowhere. Life and leadership are the same.

KATHERINE GRAINGER

Small misalignments affect collective progress. Timing, rhythm and cooperation are as important as individual strength.

- Which team members out of sync with others?
- How do you help athletes adjust to each other?
- What strategies could you use to keep everyone in the same direction?

TWENTY-SEVEN

> Details matter. If we're casual in the small things, we'll
> be casual when it counts.

SARAH ULMER

Casual habits in low-stakes moments seep into high-pressure situations. The way you do anything is how you do everything.

- Which area of the program feel too casual?
- What small detail would you like to tighten ?
- How can you model importance of details to others?

TWENTY-EIGHT

> You can accomplish anything you want as long as you
> don't care who gets the credit for it.

BLANTON COLLIER

When success matters more than recognition. Teams built on this attitude share praise and stay focused on collective goals.

- Where does the need for credit show up in your environment?
- How do you recognise contributions in ways that highlight the group, not just individuals?
- What can you say or do to reinforce that shared success matters more than personal highlights?

TWENTY-NINE

 When the locker room is strong, the scoreboard usually follows.

BECKY HAMMON

The quality of relationships, standards and conversations in shared spaces shapes performance when the whistle blows.

- What is the mood and standards in your locker room?
- What behaviors help or undermine performance?
- What small change to your pre- or post-game routines could strengthen that environment?

THIRTY

 In gymnastics, every finger, every toe is part of the performance. That's how I want my team to think about their habits.

SHANNON MILLER

Treat every aspect of preparation as meaningful. Minor technical or lifestyle choices all add up and effect the outcome.

- Which small habits would change outcomes if consistently improved?
- How do you help athletes understand the link between daily choices and performance?
- What is one habit you want your group to work on?

THIRTY-ONE

> You don't always control the outcome, but you always control your response.

NICOLA ADAMS

Coaching directly influences athletes reactions to calls, errors and events they cannot control.

- Where do athletes give away energy by reacting poorly?
- How do you coach emotional responses after tough calls or mistakes?
- What cues could help your group to choose their response?

THIRTY-TWO

> We told our runners to hold on for 30 minutes of agony for 12 months of glory.

JOHN MCDONNELL

Helping athletes connect present pain with future meaning can trigger perseverance.

- How do you frame intense efforts so athletes see the bigger picture?
- Where might your group be backing off just when it matters most to push?
- What is your experience of discomfort that paid off later?

THIRTY-THREE

> For me, coaching is about helping people believe in possibilities they can't yet see.

STACEY MARINKOVICH

Defines coaching as expanding belief. Athletes often need someone to hold a larger vision for them until they can own it themselves.

- Which athlete currently needs you to believe in them more than they believe in themselves?
- How do you communicate belief genuinely?
- What is one practical way you can show an athlete what is possible for them?

THIRTY-FOUR

> I tell the players: your legacy is how you make your teammates better.

TARA VANDERVEER

Shifts the idea of legacy from within, to impact on others. Great players elevate those around (with attitude, effort and example).

- How do you define legacy within your team or program?
- Who currently makes others better, and how could you highlight their influence?
- What questions challenge leaders to think more about their impact?

THIRTY-FIVE

 You don't have to be best friends, but you do have to respect each other and play for each other.

STACEY MARINKOVICH

Effective teams need respect and commitment over constant harmony. Professionalism and goals can bridge personal differences.

- Where do personal differences get in the way of performance?
- How do you set expectations around respect and behavior between teammates?
- What would strengthen play for each other mentality?

THIRTY-SIX

 Things are not going to get easier. You are going to handle hard better.

KARA LAWSON

Reframes development as increasing capacity. As standards rise, the goal is to grow athletes' ability to cope with pressure and difficulty.

- How do you help athletes recognise how far their capacity has already grown?
- Where might you be protecting players from difficulty?
- What training or conversations could better prepare your group to handle hard next season?

THIRTY-SEVEN

 Focus on doing the next thing right; the score takes care of itself.

LISA ALEXANDER

Encourages attention to immediate actions rather than focus on the scoreboard. When focus narrows appropriately, performance and calm both improve.

- When pressure rises, what do your athletes tend to focus on, the score or next action?
- How do you break games or routines?
- What cues or processes can help reset to the next job?

THIRTY-EIGHT

 The absolute bottom line in coaching is organization and preparing for practice.

BILL WALSH

The quality of practice design underpins everything. Thoughtful planning, clear structure and effective drills creates improvement.

- How much time do you devote to planning versus running sessions?
- Where could your training be more intentional?
- What one change to your preparation process would most improve practice quality?

THIRTY-NINE

 We win when 'I' becomes 'we' in every conversation, every huddle, every training session.

CARLA OVERBECK

Highlights language and mindset as indicators of culture. Frequent 'we' talk reflects genuine shared ownership of goals and outcomes.

- How often do you hear 'I' versus 'we'?
- How do you shift conversations toward 'we' language?
- How might you reinforce shared ownership when things go wrong or right?

FORTY

 Pressure is a privilege. It only comes to those who earn it.

MIKE KRZYZEWSKI

Pressure is evidence of opportunity and achievement. Athletes who see big moments as privilege are more likely to embrace them.

- How do your athletes currently talk about pressure situations?
- What stories could you share that show pressure as a sign of trust and respect?
- How might you prepare your group to welcome pressure rather than fear it?

FORTY-ONE

Negativity can slip into your daily activities, but a positive attitude will win your battles.

NICK BOLLETTIERI

Warns that negative thinking can erode confidence and effort. Managing inner dialogue becomes part of performance work.

- Where does negativity most often creep into your team's day: language, body-language, humour?
- How do you personally influence the emotional tone of training and competition?
- What simple practices could help athletes redirect unhelpful thoughts more quickly?

FORTY-TWO

The little things make the big things happen.

HERB BROOKS

Links small, consistent actions with major outcomes. Technical detail, discipline and preparation creates the platform for success.

- What little things do you insist on, and why do they matter?
- Where have you seen a small habit lead to a big result?
- What new small behavior would you like your group to adopt before your next big event?

FORTY-THREE

 A successful team beats with one heart.

ALEX FERGUSON

Speaks to unity of purpose and emotional connection. Through connection, effort, decision-making and resilience align.

- How aligned is your team?
- What events, stories or rituals could strengthen a sense of shared heart?
- How do you respond when behavior is out of sync?

FORTY-FOUR

 The secret to coaching is not what you know, but what your players have learned.

RED AUERBACH

Shifts focus from coach knowledge to player understanding and transfer. A measure of success is what athletes can do independently.

- How do you currently gauge what your athletes have learned?
- Where might you be talking too much and checking for understanding too little?
- What could you change in your sessions so players do more of the explaining and demonstrating?

FORTY-FIVE

Good teams become great ones when the members trust each other enough to surrender the 'me' for the 'we'.

PHIL JACKSON

Describes moving from cooperation to sacrifice. Great teams will trade personal comfort, minutes or stats for the collective good.

- Where do you see athletes choosing 'me' over 'we'?
- How do you acknowledge sacrifices for the team?
- What standards could help clarify 'surrendering me'?

FORTY-SIX

Coaches who can outline plays on a blackboard are a dime a dozen. The ones who win get inside their players and motivate.

VINCE LOMBARDI

Differentiates technical knowledge from emotional connection. Athletes feel understood, inspired and driven from within.

- How much time do you spend understanding your athletes compared with designing tactics?
- What motivates each player beyond winning itself?
- What could you do this week to better understand your athletes and connect with what drives them?

FORTY-SEVEN

Everybody makes mistakes, that's why they put erasers on pencils.

TOMMY LASORDA

Normalises errors helping to reduce fear and tension. Learning around mistakes can unlock freer, more creative play.

- How serious is your environment when someone makes an error?
- What example could you share of a mistake that later became a turning point?
- How might you respond next time showing errors are for learning, not labelling?

FORTY-EIGHT

If you command wisely, you'll be obeyed cheerfully.

THOMAS FULLER

Links leadership style with athlete buy-in. Wise, fair and clear direction encourages willing effort rather than reluctant compliance.

- How clear and consistent are your expectations?
- Where might athletes experience your instructions as reactive rather than responsive?
- What changes to your communication would make it easier for players to follow you gladly?

FORTY-NINE

> The most valuable player is the one that makes the most players valuable.

PEYTON MANNING

Redefines value as impact on others rather than individual statistics. True leaders multiply the performance and confidence of teammates.

- Who on your team currently makes others better?
- How do you encourage emerging leaders to think about lifting teammates, not just themselves?
- What feedback could you give a key player about how their behavior affects the group?

FIFTY

> Everyone wants to win, but not everyone is willing to prepare to win.

BOBBY KNIGHT

Draws a sharp line between desire and preparation. The real separator is who is willing to do the unglamorous work consistently.

- Where is there a gap between what your group says it wants and how it prepares?
- What parts of preparation do athletes most resist?
- How can you athletes connect preparation more clearly to the outcomes they desire?

FIFTY-ONE

 If you don't have time to do it right, when will you have time to do it over?

JOHN WOODEN

Challenges rushed, careless work and advocates for quality from the start. Doing things properly saves time, energy and confidence later.

- Where are you accepting near enough in your coaching or your athletes' habits?
- How could better planning or organisation give you time to do things right?
- What is one area you will slow down in now to avoid fixing it later?

FIFTY-TWO

 Hard work beats talent when talent doesn't work hard.

TIM NOTKE

Elevates effort and attitude above ability, especially over the long term. Consistent work closes talent gaps and can defy expectations.

- Who currently relies heavily on talent without the work?
- How do you spotlight players whose effort outpaces ability?
- What messages and structures could further embed a hard work first mindset in your team?

OTHER QUOTES TO INSPIRE

Use this section to collect quotes that inspire you throughout the year. Add a few notes about why each quote stands out or what it means to you personally.

The Quotivation Series is a collection of reflective quote journals designed to take short bites of wisdom, and applying it in a practical way to your upcoming success.

Quotes for Athletes: *A weekly journal of quotes for grit, motivation and a winning mindset.*

Quotes for Coaches: *A weekly journal of quotes for leadership, motivation and excellence.*

Quotes for Referees: *A weekly journal of quotes for focus, poise and resilience.*

Quotes for Business: *A weekly journal of quotes for strategy, growth and success.*

Quotes for Leaders: *A weekly journal of quotes for vision, courage, and inspired achievement.*

Quotes for Investors: *A weekly journal of quotes for patience, clarity and a successful investors mindset.*

Quotes for Military: *A weekly journal of quotes for courage, discipline, and an unbreakable mindset in service.*

Quotes for Parenting: *A weekly journal of quotes for patience, guidance, and love.*

Quotes for Students: *A weekly journal of quotes for focus, persistence and curiosity.*

Quotes for You: *A weekly journal of quotes for growth, self-discovery, and an empowered mindset.*

The Quotivation Series is being released through 2026.
Visit my website **drjolukins.com** to be the first to order your copy or visit your preferred indie bookstore or online platform.

The following books are available at your favourite book store or online platform:

The Elite: Think like an athlete, succeed like a champion. Ten things the elite do differently. 2019

In the Grandstands: The sporting parents guide to raising a confident and happy teen in the highs and lows of youth sports. 2020

The Game Plan: Your 5-month coaching program to champion high performance habits (High Performance Thinking). 2022

The Elite and The Game Plan 2 in 1 Book: Champion your success with elite habits to unleash your winning potential with 10 proven strategies and high-performance coaching program. 2023

Belief: Building unshakeable confidence. 2024

The Whistle Blower: The mental toughness rulebook for referees, umpires, and sports officials. 2025.

The Whistle Blower Workbook: The mental toughness rulebook for referees, umpires, and sports officials. 2025

Referred to as a psychological Indiana Jones, thanks to more than twenty-five years spent exploring what helps people achieve their best. I have enjoyed bringing together these quotes for you. If you'd like to connect or learn more, you can always find me at www.drjolukins.com.

If Quotes for Coaches has made an impact for you, I'd be grateful if you would share your thoughts or leave a review on Amazon or Goodreads. Similarly, if you'd like to share your favorite quote with me, let me know at excel@drjolukins.com

Shine Bright, Dr. Jo